Teacher Training Reforms Under NEP 2020

Priyanka Verma

DIAMOND BOOKS

www.diamondbooks.in

Publisher	:	**Diamond Pocket Books (P) Ltd.** X-30, Okhla Industrial Area, Phase-II New Delhi-110020
Phone	:	011-40712200
E-mail	:	wecare@diamondbooks.in
Website	:	www.diamondbooks.in
Edition	:	2025
Printed By	:	Repro (India)

Preface

Welcome to "Teach Smart, Teach Right", a practical guide created for teachers who are not just teaching for today—but shaping India's future.

The National Education Policy (NEP) 2020 is a historic and transformational reform. It redefines education in India—making it child-centered, competency-based, and deeply rooted in Indian values and global outlook. But for this reform to come alive, it must begin where real learning happens—in the classroom.

This handbook is not a policy commentary. It's a daily-use resource filled with tips, tools, strategies, and real-world examples. Whether you are a seasoned educator, a new teacher, or a school leader, this book will help you translate NEP 2020 into everyday teaching practices—simply and powerfully.

You'll find short chapters, checklists, "Try This" activities, and reflective tasks you can use today, not someday. It's written in plain language—just like how we speak in our staff rooms and share ideas.
So pick a chapter, try a tip, and take the first step in your NEP journey.
Together, let's teach smarter. Let's teach right.

- Priyanka Verma

Foreword

Education is the backbone of any progressive nation, and teachers are the architects of that future.
India's National Education Policy 2020 calls for a reimagined classroom—one that is joyful, inclusive, and rooted in 21st-century skills. But no reform—no matter how visionary—can succeed without empowering the people who will implement it: our teachers.

This handbook, *Teach Smart, Teach Right,* is a timely and practical response to that call.
It reflects the essence of NEP 2020—not just in policy, but in real classroom application. From understanding the 5+3+3+4 structure to building foundational literacy, integrating technology, using activity-based learning, and fostering inclusive classrooms—this book covers it all in simple, actionable ways.

I congratulate the authors and contributors for creating a guide that speaks to the teacher, for the teacher, and most importantly, with the teacher.
As you turn these pages, may you find not just strategies—but inspiration.
Let us walk together in this journey to make classrooms meaningful, learning joyful, and teaching powerful.

Table of Contents

Chapter 1

Understanding NEP 2020

What Every Teacher Must Know

Objective of the Chapter

To help teachers grasp the essential ideas of India's National Education Policy (NEP) 2020 in simple terms and begin thinking about how these reforms impact day-to-day teaching.

Why Should You Care About NEP 2020?

You're standing at the center of the biggest education reform India has seen in over 30 years. The NEP 2020 is not just another policy—it's a new way of thinking about children, learning, and schools. This policy puts the teacher at the heart of meaningful change.

You're not just delivering content anymore. You are shaping young minds, helping students become thoughtful citizens, and preparing them for a fast-changing world.

What Is NEP 2020, In Simple Words?

The National Education Policy 2020 is India's official roadmap to transform education. Here's what it aims to do:

- Make learning more fun, engaging, and useful
- Move away from rote memorization to real understanding
- Focus on skills, not just facts
- Introduce foundational literacy and numeracy (FLN) in early years
- Promote multilingualism and Indian languages
- Reduce exam stress with continuous and competency-based assessments
- Make teachers autonomous, respected, and professionally supported

The policy is child-centric, teacher-empowering, and future-oriented.

The New 5+3+3+4 Structure – What It Means for You

The old 10+2 system is gone. NEP introduces a new structure based on how children grow:

Stage	Age Group	Grades	Focus Area
Foundational	3–8 years	Pre-K to Grade 2	Play-based learning, FLN
Preparatory	8–11 years	Grades 3–5	Discovery and activity-based learning
Middle	11–14 years	Grades 6–8	Subject-based, experiential learning
Secondary	14–18 years	Grades 9–12	Critical thinking, flexibility, deeper study

Instead of forcing content early, the new system respects child development. You are expected to teach in ways that match your students' age, interests, and abilities.

From Teaching to Learning: A Big Shift

Let's compare how classrooms are changing:

Old Approach	New NEP Way
Teacher speaks, student listens	Student asks, explores, and learns
Focus on textbooks	Focus on concepts and real-life use
Exams decide everything	Learning is continuous and seen in many ways
Language is rigid	Local languages and bilingual tools encouraged
Syllabus completion is the goal	Understanding is the goal

NEP 2020 invites you to become a facilitator, not just a lecturer. The job is not to "cover the book," but to help students uncover meaning.

5 Quick Ways to Align with NEP – Start Today!

You don't need a new degree or expensive tools. Small changes can make a big impact.

1. Ask Open-Ended Questions
Instead of "What is the capital of India?", try:
"Why do we need a capital city?"

2. Use Local Examples
Teaching area? Use your classroom size. Teaching pollution? Talk about a nearby river.

3. Allow Student Voice
Let students ask questions, present summaries, or explain concepts in their own words.

4. Replace Some Lectures with Activities
A simple group task, role play, or drawing can make a concept stick.

5. Reflect Often
At the end of each day or week, ask yourself:
- What worked well?
- What did students struggle with?
- What can I try differently?

NEP-Inspired Class Snapshot

Here's how a typical classroom could look with NEP in action:

Time	Activity	NEP Focus
5 mins	Ask a thought-provoking question	Critical thinking
15 mins	Teach with examples and visuals	Concept clarity
15 mins	Group discussion or activity	Peer learning
10 mins	Student reflection or journaling	Self-awareness and expression

It's not about doing more, but doing it differently.

Watch Out: Common Pitfalls to Avoid

✗ Don't Overload Content: NEP promotes understanding, not overstuffed lessons.
✗ Don't Punish Curiosity: Questions mean learning is happening—

encourage them.
✗ Don't Rely Only on Exams: Use quizzes, projects, discussions, and portfolios.

Try This: One-Day NEP Lesson Plan

Here's a simple template to transform one of your lessons:

Element	What to Do
Topic	"Sources of Water"
Start	Ask: "What would life be like with no rain for a year?"
Teach	Use images, videos, and real stories
Activity	Have students create a water map of their area
Wrap-Up	Quick quiz + student reflections

The Role of the Teacher in NEP: You Are the Change

NEP 2020 trusts teachers. It gives you the power to make your classroom joyful, relevant, and inclusive.

You're not just delivering chapters. You're shaping:
• Thinkers who can question the world
• Doers who apply what they learn
• Citizens who respect others and their roots
That's why your role has never been more important.

Reflective Journal Prompt

Take 10 minutes after school today and write:
• What is one thing I learned about NEP today?
• Which classroom practice do I already do well?
• What small change can I try tomorrow?

Chapter Summary

- NEP 2020 focuses on child development, competency, and joyful learning.
- The 5+3+3+4 structure aligns with how children grow.
- You are expected to become a facilitator, not just a content provider.
- Small steps—like open questions, visuals, and peer learning—can bring NEP to life.
- Reflect, adapt, and grow as a teacher each week.

Chapter 2

The Teacher's Role in the New India

Objective of the Chapter

To help teachers understand how their professional identity is evolving under NEP 2020—from a traditional "giver of knowledge" to a facilitator, mentor, and reflective practitioner who prepares students for life and lifelong learning.

Let's Begin: Teachers as Nation Builders

In the past, you may have heard the phrase: "A teacher touches eternity." NEP 2020 makes this even more true.
As India reimagines its classrooms, the teacher becomes the centre of change. You're not only guiding academic success—but shaping character, values, curiosity, confidence, and citizenship.

NEP 2020 does not add more burden on you. Instead, it offers more flexibility, more creativity, and more professional respect. It believes that teachers are leaders—not workers following a script.

From Instructor to Facilitator: The Shift

Old Role	NEP Role
Deliver textbook content	Design engaging, flexible lessons
Focus on finishing syllabus	Focus on developing competencies
Prepare for one exam	Support continuous learning
Authority figure	Learning partner and mentor
Works alone	Collaborates with colleagues and parents

This shift doesn't mean losing control—it means gaining more power to shape learning in ways that actually work.

Who Is the "NEP Teacher"?

NEP envisions a teacher who is:

- **Student-centered:** Thinks about how students learn best

- **Inclusive:** Welcomes all learners—regardless of ability, background, or language

- **Reflective:** Learns from experience and adapts accordingly

- **Innovative:** Uses new tools, strategies, and real-life examples

- **Empathetic:** Understands the emotional world of students

- **Collaborative:** Builds relationships with other teachers, parents, and the community

5 Habits of the NEP-Ready Teacher

1. Curate, Don't Just Deliver

You don't have to teach everything in the textbook. Choose what matters, connect it to real life, and simplify it with relatable stories and tools.

2. Make Learning Visible

Ask students to show what they've learned through charts, stories, projects, or discussion. Let them express understanding in their own ways.

3. Encourage Thinking, Not Just Answering

Use open-ended questions:

"What do you think?"

"Why might that happen?"

"How would you solve this?"

4. Reflect Every Week

Take 15 minutes each week to write:

- One thing that worked
- One thing that didn't
- One thing you'd like to try next week

5. Celebrate Mistakes

If a child gets an answer wrong but tries hard—applaud the effort. This builds confidence and creates a fearless learning space.

Quick Checklist: Are You Teaching the NEP Way?

Yes/No	Practice
	I let students ask and explore, not just listen

	I use stories, visuals, or activities regularly
	I speak to students with patience and empathy
	I reflect on my teaching style each week
	I work with parents or peers to improve learning

If you answered "yes" to 3 or more, you're already on the NEP path!

TRY THIS: Redesign Your Class for a Day

Choose any one subject and follow this outline:

Element	Strategy
Start	Ask a real-life question: "Why does salt dissolve in water?"
Teach	Use props (glass of water, spoon, salt) and let students guess and observe
Explore	Group task: Try dissolving other materials (sugar, oil, etc.)
Reflect	Ask students to explain findings in their notebooks or aloud
Extend	Ask: "Where do you see this happen in real life?"

Even in a 35-minute period, students will understand deeply and joyfully.

DO'S AND DON'TS OF A NEW-AGE TEACHER

Do	Don't
Use your voice to inspire, not to command	Shout or shame students
Let students lead discussions or groups	Lecture from start to finish
Admit when you don't know something	Pretend to know everything
Build habits for life (respect, curiosity, teamwork)	Focus only on test preparation
Keep learning—just like your students	Believe training ends after your degree

ASK YOURSELF: Teacher as Lifelong Learner

When was the last time I learned something new—about teaching, children, or a subject?
Learning never ends. Even a short webinar, staff-room discussion, or reflective journal helps you grow.

Try This in the Staff Room

Form a peer circle of 2–3 teachers.

Each week:

- Share one success story from your classroom
- Share one challenge you're facing
- Suggest one new strategy for each other

This kind of Professional Learning Community (PLC) is recommended by NEP 2020 as a tool for teacher growth and motivation.

Reflective Journal Prompt

After your next class, reflect on:

- How much time did students spend actively learning vs. listening?
- Did you encourage questions or creativity?
- What would you like to try differently tomorrow?

Chapter Summary

- NEP 2020 views teachers as facilitators, guides, and mentors
- Your role is to build curiosity, confidence, and competencies—not just marks
- You must balance content delivery with real-world relevance
- Use reflection, peer support, and student feedback as growth tools
- Every teacher can lead change—one child, one lesson at a time

Chapter 3

The 5+3+3+4 Curriculum Explained Simply

Objective of the Chapter

To help teachers understand India's new school structure under NEP 2020—how it's different from the old 10+2 model, what each stage focuses on, and how to align classroom practices with a child's development needs.

Let's Begin: Why the Change?

Have you ever felt like your students were too young or too old for a particular lesson? That's because learning is not just about grades—it's about how the brain grows, how children absorb knowledge, and how they engage with the world.

NEP 2020 recognizes this and introduces a new curricular structure called 5+3+3+4. It replaces the outdated 10+2 system with something that matches how children actually grow and learn.

What Is the 5+3+3+4 Structure?

This new model breaks the school years into four key developmental stages:

Stage	Age Group	Grades	Focus
Foundational	3–8 years	Pre-K to Grade 2	Play, storytelling, early literacy and numeracy
Preparatory	8–11 years	Grades 3–5	Activity-based learning, exploration, language development
Middle	11–14 years	Grades 6–8	Subject learning, critical thinking, projects
Secondary	14–18 years	Grades 9–12	Flexibility, deeper learning, career readiness

What's Different from the Old System?

Old (10+2)	New (5+3+3+4)
Focused mainly on subjects	Focused on how children learn
Emphasized exams	Emphasizes competencies
Treated K–12 as one block	Divides based on cognitive development

Uniform teaching for all Encourages age-appropriate pedagogy This shift encourages you as a teacher to adapt your style to fit the learner, not force the learner to fit the style.

Foundational Stage (Pre-K to Grade 2 | Ages 3–8)

What to Know:

- Children are learning through senses, play, and imitation
- Language is developing fast—use rhymes, pictures, and actions

How to Teach:

- Prioritize foundational literacy and numeracy (FLN)
- Avoid long lectures—use songs, puzzles, play-based tasks
- Create a warm, joyful classroom environment

NEP Tip: Use storybooks, objects, and roleplay instead of heavy textbooks.

Preparatory Stage (Grades 3–5 | Ages 8–11)

What to Know:

- Children begin to develop logic and curiosity
- They enjoy hands-on activities and asking "why?"

How to Teach:

- Use projects, posters, science experiments
- Introduce basic subject knowledge in an active, fun way
- Use local examples to explain abstract topics

NEP Tip: One activity per lesson keeps students engaged and improves retention.

Middle Stage (Grades 6–8 | Ages 11–14)

What to Know:

- Students start developing their own opinions and identity
- They are ready for abstract and interdisciplinary learning

How to Teach:

• Introduce critical thinking and reasoning tasks
• Encourage peer learning through debates, group projects, and roleplay
• Blend digital tools with traditional methods

NEP Tip: Allow students to ask big questions and investigate answers themselves.

Secondary Stage (Grades 9–12 | Ages 14–18)

What to Know:
• Students want relevance: "Why am I learning this?"
• This is the time for deep learning, choice, and reflection

How to Teach:
• Shift to project-based learning, case studies, and fieldwork
• Allow subject choice (art, coding, science, social work, etc.)
• Focus on building career awareness and life skills

NEP Tip: Use real-world examples and problems to teach concepts meaningfully.

TRY THIS: Match Your Lesson to the Stage

Stage	Subject	Example
Foundational	Math	Use beads to teach counting
Preparatory	Science	Plant a seed and observe growth
Middle	History	Roleplay a freedom movement scene
Secondary	English	Debate on social media's impact

When teaching matches how kids grow, learning becomes natural.

Quick Checklist for Stage-Wise Alignment

Yes/No	Do You...
	Know which NEP stage your students are in?
	Plan your teaching methods based on their age group?
	Include sensory or physical activities for younger students?
	Use real-life and peer activities for older students?
	Reflect on stage-fit teaching after class?

If you answered "yes" to 3 or more—you're on the right path.

PRO TIPS for Each Stage

Stage	Pro Tip
Foundational	Use circle time, visuals, and hands-on toys daily
Preparatory	Turn lessons into games or mini-projects
Middle	Encourage questions and independent work
Secondary	Give students real-world problems to solve

DO'S & DON'TS of Stage-Based Teaching

Do	Don't
Teach based on age and ability	Use the same method for all grades
Make learning fun and relatable	Overload with textbook content
Let students move, talk, create	Expect silence all the time

Give choices and encourage dialogue	Discourage questions or doubt

Reflective Journal Prompt

Think about your last class:

- Did your method match your students' age and stage?
- Were they engaged or distracted?
- What one change can you try next class to improve alignment?

Chapter Summary

- The 5+3+3+4 system is based on how children grow and learn best
- Each stage (Foundational, Preparatory, Middle, Secondary) has different learning needs
- NEP encourages age-appropriate pedagogy, not one-size-fits-all teaching
- Match your teaching style to each stage for better engagement and outcomes
- Reflect often, adjust your strategies, and keep evolving with your learners

Chapter 4

Foundational Literacy & Numeracy (FLN)

Objective of the Chapter

To help teachers understand the concept of FLN (Foundational Literacy and Numeracy), why it is central to NEP 2020, and how they can strengthen early reading, writing, and number skills through simple daily practices.

What Is FLN?

Foundational Literacy and Numeracy (FLN) refers to a child's ability to read with understanding, write clearly, and perform basic math operations such as counting, addition, and subtraction by the end of Grade 3.

Without these basic skills, children struggle to progress in school and often lose interest in learning. NEP 2020 identifies FLN as the most urgent and critical goal in early education.

Why FLN Matters

Imagine trying to solve a science problem if you can't read the instructions. Or managing your money without understanding numbers.

FLN isn't just about reading and math—it's about:

- Confidence in learning
- School retention
- Daily life skills
- Equity in education

According to surveys, many children in India reach Grade 5 without being able to read Grade 2-level text or do basic calculations. FLN aims to change this.

The NIPUN Bharat Mission

To make FLN a reality, the Government of India launched the NIPUN Bharat (National Initiative for Proficiency in Reading with Understanding and Numeracy) mission in 2021.

Goal: Achieve universal FLN by Grade 3 for all children by 2026–27

As a teacher, you are a key FLN warrior. Your efforts in the first five years of schooling make the biggest difference.

What Are the Core FLN Skills?

Foundational Literacy

- Listening comprehension
- Vocabulary development
- Phonemic awareness (understanding sounds)
- Letter-sound recognition
- Reading fluency

• Writing simple words and sentences

Foundational Numeracy
• Number sense (counting, comparing, grouping)
• Number operations (addition, subtraction)
• Shapes and measurements
• Understanding patterns and sequences

5 Ways to Build FLN in Your Classroom

1. Read Aloud Daily
Reading to children every day builds vocabulary, curiosity, and comprehension. Use picture books, folk tales, and poems. Add actions and expressions to make it fun!

2. Use Sound and Syllables
Before children learn to read words, they must understand sounds.

Play games like:
• Clap the syllables in their names
• Find rhyming words
• Identify beginning and ending sounds

3. Use Objects for Math
Use local materials—stones, sticks, bottle caps—to teach counting and addition. This builds understanding through touch and movement.

4. Turn Class into a Language Lab
Encourage storytelling, role play, question-answer sessions, and show-and-tell. Children who speak more, read more, and write more.

5. Make Mistakes Normal
Praise effort, not perfection. Let children experiment with letters and numbers. Celebrate progress in small steps.

TRY THIS: A One-Week FLN Boost Plan

Day	Literacy Focus	Numeracy Focus
Monday	Read a story and discuss characters	Count classroom items
Tuesday	Match letter sounds with pictures	Add using bottle caps
Wednesday	Sing rhyming poems	Draw and compare shapes
Thursday	Word wall: Add 5 new words	Number line hopping
Friday	Write 3 sentences about a picture	Practice subtraction with fingers

Even 30–40 minutes a day can have a lasting impact.

Tools and Materials You Can Use

Literacy Tools	Numeracy Tools
Flashcards	Counters, pebbles
Charts and posters	Number lines
Sand tray for tracing letters	Dominoes
Storybooks	Dice, sticks
Puppet and picture cards	Shapes and puzzle sets

NEP Tip: Use materials that are low-cost, locally available, and durable.

Quick Checklist: Am I Supporting FLN?

Yes/No	Task
	I read to children daily
	I let children speak and express ideas
	I use songs or games to teach sounds and numbers
	I give children time to explore letters and numbers on their own
	I encourage learning through play

If you checked at least 3 boxes—you're helping build FLN!

DO'S & DON'TS FOR FLN TEACHERS

DO	DON'T
Use the child's home language to build early literacy	Force English reading too early
Focus on understanding, not speed	Rush through the syllabus
Repeat stories and games often	Introduce too many concepts at once
Encourage children to guess and experiment	Correct every small mistake harshly

Reflective Journal Prompt

At the end of the week, ask yourself:

- Which FLN activity did my students enjoy the most?
- Who is still struggling with basic skills? Why?
- What can I do differently next week?

Write down 1 success and 1 challenge.

Chapter Summary

- FLN means reading, writing, and basic math by Grade 3
- It is essential for success in school and life
- NEP 2020 and NIPUN Bharat make FLN a national priority
- Teachers should use stories, games, play, and hands-on materials daily
- Celebrate small progress and keep FLN joyful and inclusive

Chapter 5

Activity-Based & Experiential Learning

Objective of the Chapter

To help teachers understand the concept of activity-based and experiential learning promoted by NEP 2020, and to provide practical tools to make everyday classroom teaching hands-on, engaging, and meaningful.

Let's Begin: Why Activities Matter

Think about this: Do you remember the time you filled out a worksheet—or the time you built a volcano model in school? Children don't remember chapters. They remember experiences.

NEP 2020 encourages teachers to use activity-based and experiential learning to build real understanding—not just memorization. This method turns classrooms into labs of discovery where students do, create, and connect.

What Is Activity-Based Learning?

Activity-based learning (ABL) means students learn by doing. They participate in structured tasks that help them explore concepts through movement, observation, discussion, and hands-on creation.

Example: Instead of just explaining plant parts, ask students to bring leaves, examine them, draw them, and sort them.

What Is Experiential Learning?

Experiential learning goes deeper. It connects the real world with the classroom.

It includes:

- Field visits
- Role plays
- Experiments
- Art, music, and physical activities
- Problem-solving in local contexts

It follows a 4-step cycle:

1. Do the task (experience)
2. Reflect on it
3. Learn the concept behind it
4. Apply it to new situations

Example: Students clean their class garden and then learn about waste segregation, plant biology, or civic responsibility.

Why It Works

Benefit	Outcome
Increases engagement	Students enjoy learning
Improves retention	Concepts are understood, not memorised

Builds teamwork	Collaboration and communication improve
Promotes creativity	Students try new ideas and take risks
Makes learning inclusive	Supports different learning styles

TRY THIS: Simple Activities for Everyday Topics

Subject	Topic	Activity
English	Adjectives	"Describe the Object" game using real items
Math	Measurement	Measure school objects using handspan, scale
Science	Water Cycle	Roleplay as clouds, sun, and rain
Social Science	Community Helpers	Interview a school staff member
EVS	Cleanliness	Group activity: Clean the classroom area
Languages	Vocabulary	Word treasure hunt around the school

These take less than 20 minutes but can create lifelong learning!

Tools You Already Have

You don't need a big budget. Most ABL resources are already around you:

Material	How to Use
Paper cups, boxes	Build shapes or measure liquids
Sticks, leaves, stones	Math games, sorting, and science observation
Flashcards	Word games and memory tasks
Puppets or toys	Storytelling and role play
Newspapers	Reading practice, current events, vocabulary hunt
Classroom corners	Set up theme-based learning stations

Planning an Activity – 5 Quick Steps

1. Pick the topic – Choose a concept that can be shown or done.
2. Define the goal – What should students discover or learn?
3. Gather materials – Use local or low-cost resources.
4. Guide the activity – Let students explore, not just follow.
5. Discuss and reflect – Ask: "What did we learn? How can we use it?"

CLASSROOM TIP: Use the "See, Think, Do" Model

Step	Action
See	Show or demonstrate something related to the topic
Think	Ask students what they observed or understood
Do	Let them try it out themselves and reflect on the results

Example for Class 4 Science:

- **See:** Show video/picture of plant growth stages
- **Think:** Discuss what plants need to grow
- **Do:** Plant seeds and track growth over two weeks

DO'S AND DON'TS

DO	DON'T
Let students ask, experiment, and fail	Expect perfect answers or quick results
Use storytelling and drama often	Stick to textbook-only explanations
Let students work in pairs/ groups	Discourage peer sharing or team tasks
Include reflection after activities	Skip discussion and move on too quickly

Quick Checklist: Am I Using Activities Effectively?

Yes/No	Checkpoint
	Did I use at least one activity this week?
	Did I allow students to move, make, or explore?
	Did I include follow-up discussion or questions?
	Did I link the activity to a real-life situation?
	Did students enjoy and engage with the task?

If you answered "yes" to 3 or more—you're on the right path!

Journal Reflection Prompt

After your next class, reflect:

- What was the last activity I used?
- How did students react?
- What could I improve next time?

Try documenting one successful activity every week and share it with your colleagues!

Chapter Summary

- Activity-based and experiential learning are key pillars of NEP 2020
- They make classrooms engaging, practical, and inclusive
- You can use local, low-cost materials to plan great activities
- Simple steps—plan, guide, reflect—can transform your teaching
- Learning through experience builds life-long curiosity and confidence

Chapter 6

Using Technology & Blended Learning

Objective of the Chapter

To help teachers understand how to integrate simple, meaningful, and age-appropriate digital tools in the classroom and embrace blended learning as envisioned in NEP 2020.

Let's Begin: Technology Is a Tool, Not a Distraction

Technology is not about fancy gadgets or expensive software. It's about enhancing learning and making teaching smarter, faster, and more fun.

NEP 2020 encourages "blended learning"—a balance between traditional face-to-face methods and digital or online tools. It gives teachers the flexibility to use both chalk and click, depending on what suits the topic and the students.

What Is Blended Learning?

Blended learning is a mix of classroom teaching and digital resources. It's not about replacing teachers with screens—it's about empowering teachers with tools.

A simple example:
• You introduce a topic in class (e.g., "How rain is formed")
• Then you show a short animated video or simulation
• Students do a group worksheet, and later revise using an app or quiz online

Benefits of Using Technology in Classrooms

Benefit	Outcome
Visual learning	Better concept clarity
Immediate feedback	Faster understanding of gaps
Access to content anytime	Reinforces classroom learning
Creative expression	Students make videos, posters, stories
Inclusive learning	Audio, visual, and language support for all learners

5 Simple Ways to Use Technology as a Teacher

1. Use Educational Videos
Platforms like YouTube, DIKSHA, and Khan Academy offer short, high-quality videos in multiple languages.

Try This: Play a 3–5 minute clip and then ask students to explain what they understood.

2. Create Digital Quizzes or Polls

Use Google Forms, Kahoot, or Quizzizz for instant assessment.

Try This: End your class with a 5-question digital quiz using students' smartphones or a shared device.

3. Use WhatsApp or Telegram for Home Learning
Send simple assignments, audio stories, or worksheets to parents for at-home revision.

Try This: Record your voice reading a story and share it for children to listen at home.

4. Show Images or Simulations
Use visuals for topics like food chains, geography, body systems, or historical events.

Try This: Use Google Earth to show continents or landmarks during a geography lesson.

5. Assign Creative Tasks
Ask students to create digital posters, record interviews, or make photo essays using basic apps.

Try This: Assign a "My Community Hero" video interview using mobile phones.

Government Tools Every Teacher Should Know

Platform	Use
DIKSHA	Videos, textbooks, teaching aids in Indian languages
NISHTHA	Online teacher training modules
ePathshala	NCERT books and content
Swayam	Free online courses for students and teachers

PM eVIDYA	Multimode education including TV, radio, and digital tools

These platforms are free, multilingual, and aligned with NEP 2020.

Even Without Internet: Tech Can Still Work

Don't have smartboards or Wi-Fi? No problem. Use offline tech or low-tech options.

Tool	How to Use
Radio	Tune into educational shows (e.g., All India Radio school broadcasts)
TV	Watch PM eVIDYA programs or recorded lessons
Pre-downloaded content	Share PDFs, videos via USB or phone-to-phone transfer
Audio recordings	Use MP3 players or record voice messages for storytelling

Quick Checklist: Are You Using Blended Learning?

Yes/No	Practice
	I have used at least one digital tool in my class this week
	I showed a short video or image related to the topic
	I sent home a voice note or digital worksheet
	I used a quiz app or online test platform
	I accessed free content from DIKSHA or ePathshala

If you checked 3 or more—you're blending learning effectively!

DO'S AND DON'TS FOR EDTECH

DO	DON'T
Use tech to simplify learning	Use tech just to look modern
Make screen time short and focused	Show long videos without purpose
Ensure all students are included	Assume everyone has access
Mix tech with discussion and hands-on work	Replace all classroom activity with screens

TRY THIS: A Simple 30-Minute Blended Lesson Plan

Time	Task	Method
5 mins	Warm-up question	Teacher-led
10 mins	Watch a video or simulation	Technology
10 mins	Group discussion or drawing	Activity-based
5 mins	Quick quiz using a digital tool	Formative assessment

This plan keeps technology meaningful, limited, and engaging.

Reflective Journal Prompt

After trying a tech-enabled lesson, reflect:

- Did the tool improve student understanding?
- What challenges did I face?
- Which student seemed most engaged and why?

Write down your top 1–2 ideas for the next class.

Chapter Summary

• NEP 2020 promotes blended learning—a mix of digital and traditional teaching
• Technology should support—not replace—good teaching
• Use simple, free tools like videos, WhatsApp, DIKSHA, and quizzes
• Plan short, purposeful digital interactions
• Reflect, adapt, and be inclusive when using tech

Chapter 7

Continuous Professional Development (CPD)

Objective of the Chapter

To help teachers understand the importance of CPD as envisioned in NEP 2020, and how they can take small, consistent steps to grow their knowledge, skills, and confidence in everyday practice.

Let's Begin: Learning Never Stops

Teachers often say, "We are lifelong learners." NEP 2020 takes this seriously—and turns it into a national policy priority.
Continuous Professional Development (CPD) is not just training—it's about personal and professional growth. It ensures that teachers stay current, motivated, reflective, and empowered.

In a world that's changing fast—digitally, socially, and educationally—teachers need CPD just like doctors need regular practice updates.

What Is CPD?

CPD stands for Continuous Professional Development. It is a planned, ongoing process where teachers:

- Learn new techniques
- Reflect on their classroom practices
- Stay updated on curriculum and pedagogy
- Improve leadership and communication skills
- Collaborate with peers for better results

NEP 2020 recommends that every teacher completes at least 50 hours of CPD every year through workshops, online courses, mentoring, peer learning, and more.

Why CPD Matters

Reason	Benefit
Keeps you updated	Know the latest teaching tools and NEP strategies
Builds confidence	Handle challenges better and try new ideas
Improves student learning	Better teachers = better classrooms
Encourages reflection	Learn from what worked and what didn't
Supports career growth	Opens doors to leadership roles and mentoring

Types of CPD Activities

Not all CPD needs to happen in a formal training center. Here's a range of options:

CPD Mode	Examples
Formal training	NISHTHA modules, workshops, webinars
Peer learning	Team teaching, observing a colleague
Self-study	Reading a book, watching a teaching video
Reflection	Keeping a teaching journal or diary
Practice-based	Trying a new method and analyzing results
Community engagement	Collaborating with parents or local experts

Recommended Platforms for Free CPD

Platform	Purpose
DIKSHA	NEP-aligned training modules in multiple languages
NISHTHA	Structured CPD courses for foundational, prep, and secondary teachers
CBSE Training Portal	Online courses and certification
Swayam	Subject-specific and skill-based courses
YouTube Channels	Practical tutorials, teaching ideas, classroom hacks

These platforms offer certificates and flexible self-paced learning.

Building a Simple CPD Plan

You don't need to wait for your school to organize something. Take charge of your own development:

Step 1: Identify an area
"I want to improve group work in my classroom."

Step 2: Find resources
Watch a 10-minute video or read a blog on cooperative learning.

Step 3: Apply it in class
Try a group activity in your next period.

Step 4: Reflect
Write what worked and what didn't.

Step 5: Share
Tell a peer what you learned, and listen to their ideas.
Repeat this cycle throughout the year!

TRY THIS: Weekly CPD Routine (Just 30 mins/ week)

Day	Activity
Monday	Watch a short video on a teaching strategy
Wednesday	Reflect on a recent lesson: What could be improved?
Friday	Discuss a classroom challenge with a peer or in the staff room
Sunday	Read an article or blog on NEP or classroom techniques

Consistent micro-learning leads to macro results over time.

CPD Tracker: Keep a Simple Log

Date	Activity	Time Spent	Key Takeaway
July 2	DIKSHA Module on FLN	45 mins	Use phonics games to teach sounds

July 5	Tried project-based learning	–	Students collaborated better in groups
July 10	Watched YouTube video on class routines	15 mins	Use music for transitions

This can be digital or handwritten. You can also use Google Sheets or mobile notes.

DO'S AND DON'TS OF CPD

DO	DON'T
Choose topics that excite or challenge you	Wait for others to plan your learning
Share what you learn with others	Keep your learning to yourself
Reflect regularly	Think that one training session is enough
Explore new formats (videos, blogs, peer chats)	Stick only to lectures or PDFs
Stay curious	Think "I already know enough"

CPD Is Not One-Size-Fits-All

Some teachers prefer online modules. Others learn best through discussions or hands-on trials.
NEP 2020 supports personalized CPD—you get to choose what you need most.

Examples:

• A foundational teacher might focus on early literacy tools

• A middle school teacher might explore group projects
• A secondary teacher might dive into career guidance skills

Reflective Journal Prompt

• What's one classroom challenge I'm facing right now?
• What CPD activity could help me overcome it?
• What's my learning goal for this month?

Write your answers, and review them at the end of the term.

Chapter Summary

• CPD means learning continuously and purposefully as a teacher
• NEP 2020 recommends at least 50 hours per year
• You can learn through formal trainings, peer learning, videos, or reflective practice
• Build a simple routine, track your growth, and share with others
• A growing teacher leads to growing students

Chapter 8

Assessment Reimagined

Objective of the Chapter

To help teachers understand the shift from marks-based to learning-focused assessment under NEP 2020, and to provide simple, practical ways to assess students more meaningfully in the classroom.

Let's Begin: Is It About Scores or Skills?

Traditionally, assessments have been all about marks and exams. Students studied to score—not always to understand. NEP 2020 wants to change this.

Under the new policy, assessments must shift from:
• Testing memory → to checking understanding
• Ranking students → to supporting progress
• One big exam → to continuous, low-pressure feedback
The goal is clear: Make assessment part of learning—not the fear at the end of it.

What NEP 2020 Says About Assessment

NEP encourages "Assessment for learning," not just "Assessment of learning."

It introduces a 3-part approach:
1. Teacher Assessment – Based on classroom work and interaction
2. Peer Assessment – Students give feedback to each other
3. Self-Assessment – Students reflect on their own strengths and gaps

Together, these promote reflection, responsibility, and real growth.

What Does Good Assessment Look Like?

A meaningful assessment:
- Tells the teacher what the child understands
- Tells the child how they are progressing
- Builds confidence, not fear
- Is aligned with the learning outcomes
- Happens daily, not just during exams

Example: Instead of a test on "Types of Plants," ask students to group real leaves by features and explain their choices.

5 Simple Ways to Assess Without Exams

1. Observation

Watch how students work in groups, raise their hands, complete tasks.

Tip: Use a checklist to note if students can explain, demonstrate, and connect ideas.

2. Exit Slips

At the end of class, ask students to write one thing they learned and one question they still have.

Benefit: Takes only 5 minutes and provides real-time feedback.

3. Peer Feedback
Pair students and ask them to assess each other's projects or answers using 2 stars and 1 suggestion.
Example: "You explained the idea well, your chart is neat, but you could speak louder."

4. Portfolios
Let students collect their best work (drawings, stories, experiments) in a folder over the term.
Benefit: Shows progress, creativity, and effort.

5. Rubrics
Create a simple scoring guide. Example:

Skill: Describing an Animal	**Excellent (3)**	**Good (2)**	**Needs Work (1)**
Used 3 or more features	✔	✗	✗
Spoke clearly	✔	✔	✗
Drew the animal	✔	✗	✗

Share rubrics with students—they'll know what's expected!

TRY THIS: Assessment Tools for Different Subjects

Subject	Activity	Assessment Method
English	Storytelling	Oral fluency + creativity checklist
Math	Create a shop with prices	Observe money use + calculations

Science	Make a model	Peer assessment + explanation
Social Science	Group map-making	Rubric for teamwork and content
EVS	Observe nature walk	Reflection journal entry
Languages	Role play	Dialogue delivery + vocabulary use

Daily Assessment Checklist for Teachers

Yes/No	Practice
	I observed at least 3 students during activity time
	I asked open-ended questions to check understanding
	I used one method other than a written test this week
	I gave feedback based on effort, not just correct answers
	I allowed students to reflect on their own learning

3 or more "yes"? You're already shifting to NEP-style assessment!

DO'S AND DON'TS OF ASSESSMENT

DO	DON'T
Use different methods (drawing, discussion, group work)	Depend only on written tests
Give feedback that builds confidence	Mark answers as right/wrong without explanation

Involve students in reflection	Keep assessment a teacher-only task
Assess regularly and informally	Wait for the end of term to assess
Focus on improvement	Focus only on scores or grades

From Report Cards to Progress Cards

NEP recommends replacing one-time marksheets with Holistic Progress Cards (HPCs) that include:

- Academic progress
- Skills and interests
- Values and behavior
- Teacher + student + parent feedback

This makes reporting personal, meaningful, and well-rounded.

Tip: Keep a simple profile for each child—strengths, challenges, and best work samples.

Reflective Journal Prompt

- Did I assess students during the learning or only at the end?
- What feedback did I give that encouraged effort or creativity?
- How can I make assessment more joyful and useful next week?

Write down your answers and try one new method next class.

Chapter Summary

- NEP 2020 reimagines assessment as continuous, competency-based, and child-friendly
- Move from exams to multiple methods like observation, projects, peer review, and portfolios

- Give feedback that promotes growth and confidence
- Use rubrics, checklists, and reflection tools to make assessment clear and supportive
- Empower students with self- and peer-assessment

Chapter 9

Multilingual Classrooms Made Easy

Objective of the Chapter

To help teachers understand how to support multilingual learners, make use of students' home languages, and smoothly bridge to formal instruction in Hindi, English, or regional languages as per NEP 2020 guidelines.

Let's Begin: Many Languages, One Classroom

India is a multilingual country. A single classroom may have children who speak Hindi, Marathi, Bengali, Urdu, Tamil, Telugu, or even tribal dialects—often in the same school.
Rather than treating this as a challenge, NEP 2020 encourages teachers to embrace language diversity as a strength.
Children learn best in a language they understand. Multilingual classrooms, when handled smartly, can make learning more inclusive, more respectful, and more effective.

What NEP 2020 Says About Language

• Wherever possible, the home language/mother tongue/local language should be the medium of instruction until at least Grade 5, preferably till Grade 8.
• Children should be exposed to three languages in school.
• No language is to be imposed. Schools and teachers should follow a flexible, multilingual approach.
• Language learning should include listening, speaking, reading, and writing, with a focus on expression and understanding, not grammar alone.

Why Use the Home Language?

Benefit	Outcome
Builds confidence	Children participate more freely
Improves understanding	Concepts are clearer in familiar words
Smoothens the shift to school	Reduces dropouts and frustration
Values the child's culture	Makes children feel respected and included

Children think, feel, and dream in their home language. If we ignore that, we disconnect learning from life.

5 Practical Strategies for Multilingual Classrooms

1. Use the Child's Language to Introduce Concepts
If a student doesn't understand a word in Hindi or English, explain it in their mother tongue (if you know it) or ask a peer to help.

Example: Use a mix of English and local language: "Photosynthesis – yaani ki paudhe khud se apna khana banate hain."

2. Use Visuals, Actions, and Examples
Words are not the only way to communicate.

Use:
• Pictures, charts, and maps
• Role play and gestures
• Real objects and demonstrations

Try This: Teach "directions" using a school map and student movement instead of language-heavy explanations.

3. Encourage Peer Learning
Group students with different language backgrounds and let them help each other. Many will naturally become helpers and translators for their peers.

Example: Let a fluent child explain an activity to a new student in their home language.

4. Create a Multilingual Word Wall
Display important words in two or three languages. Update it regularly.

Example:
• "Water – पानी – Neeru"
• "Tree – पेड़ – Maram"

This helps all learners build vocabulary and shows respect for multiple languages.

5. Use Songs and Stories in Multiple Languages
Stories, rhymes, and folk songs can be a powerful multilingual tool.

Try This: Teach a Hindi rhyme, then invite a student to share a similar one in their language.

TRY THIS: Simple Multilingual Activities

Activity	Goal
Story Relay	Start a story in one language, continue in another
Word Hunt	Students find 3 objects and name them in 2 languages
Role Play	Act out scenes using home and school language
Greeting Game	Students teach greetings from their native tongue
Bilingual Reading	Read a sentence in two languages and ask the meaning

These games encourage inclusion, language learning, and joy!

Checklist: Am I Supporting a Multilingual Classroom?

Yes/No	Practice
	I allow children to express ideas in their home language
	I use visuals and gestures to support understanding
	I display key words in more than one language
	I ask bilingual students to support peers
	I use songs/stories from different cultures

If you checked 3 or more—you are creating an inclusive language environment!

DO'S AND DON'TS FOR MULTILINGUAL TEACHING

DO	DON'T
Respect all languages in the classroom	Force only one language from Day 1
Use language as a bridge, not a barrier	Laugh at or correct dialects harshly
Build connections between languages	Expect instant fluency in Hindi or English
Let students use familiar terms	Penalize children for using home language
Celebrate language diversity	Ignore the language challenges some children face

Understanding the Three-Language Formula

NEP 2020 promotes a flexible three-language formula:

1. Home language/local language – for conceptual understanding
2. Regional/state language – to connect with society
3. Hindi or English or another Indian language – for wider communication

Remember: The choice of languages is not fixed—it should be based on local needs and child comfort.

Real-Life Example

In a classroom in Karnataka:

- The teacher introduces a topic in Kannada
- Then she switches to English for keywords
- Students are encouraged to explain the concept in Tulu or Urdu, if needed

• The activity ends with a drawing and a short oral presentation in any language

Result: All students feel seen, heard, and involved.

Reflective Journal Prompt

• Which child in my class is struggling with the language of instruction?
• Have I used any of the child's home language to support learning?
• What's one multilingual strategy I can try this week?

Chapter Summary

• NEP 2020 promotes multilingual classrooms where the home language is valued
• Children learn better when they understand the language used in class
• Use visuals, peer support, word walls, and bilingual instruction
• Avoid language shaming and promote inclusion through respect
• Build bridges—not walls—with language

Chapter 10

Teaching 21st-Century Skills

Objective of the Chapter

To help teachers understand what 21st-century skills are, why they matter in today's world, and how to nurture them in everyday classroom practice—through simple, practical, NEP-aligned strategies.

Let's Begin: Are We Teaching for Today or for Tomorrow?

The world is changing rapidly—technology, jobs, and life itself are not what they were 10 years ago. Our children are entering a world where rote learning is not enough. They need to think, adapt, communicate, and solve problems creatively.

NEP 2020 clearly says: Education must equip students with 21st-century skills—not just subject knowledge, but the ability to use it in real-life situations.

What Are 21st-Century Skills?

NEP 2020 highlights four core skill areas often called the 4Cs:

Skill	**What It Means**
Critical Thinking	Asking questions, analyzing, and making decisions
Creativity	Thinking of new ideas, expressing them in different ways
Collaboration	Working well with others, sharing tasks, respecting opinions

Communication Expressing thoughts clearly—spoken, written, visual
It also includes digital literacy, emotional intelligence, problem-solving, ethics, and adaptability.

Why Teach These Skills in School?

Reason	**Impact**
Prepares for life and work	Students will face jobs that don't exist yet
Builds confidence and independence	Learners become decision-makers
Improves understanding	Students think deeper, not just faster
Encourages inclusivity	Everyone brings different strengths to a team
Aligns with NEP goals	Promotes holistic and multidisciplinary education

NEP Tip: Skills should be taught through subjects, not separately.

Simple Ways to Build 21st-Century Skills in Class

1. Ask Open-Ended Questions
Instead of "What is the capital of India?",

ask:
"If you could move the capital, where would you place it and why?"
This builds critical thinking and creativity.

2. Group Projects and Tasks
Assign roles: leader, writer, speaker, time-keeper. Let them work together and present findings.
Example: "Design your own animal with features that help it survive."

3. Think-Pair-Share
Give students a question. Let them think silently, then discuss with a partner, then share with the class.
This improves communication and confidence.

4. Debates and Role Play
Take real-world issues: "Should mobile phones be allowed in school?"
Assign teams and let them research, argue, and reflect.

5. Use Daily Journaling

Ask students to write reflections:
- What did I learn today?
- What did I struggle with?
- What would I do differently?

This builds self-awareness and emotional intelligence.

TRY THIS: Skill-Integrated Activities

Subject	Activity	Skill Focus
English	Write a new ending to a story	Creativity, Writing
Math	Solve a real-life budgeting problem	Critical Thinking
Science	Build a water filter model	Collaboration, Innovation
Social Science	Conduct a mock election	Leadership, Communication
EVS	Design a poster for water conservation	Visual Communication
Arts	Create a short play	Expression, Teamwork

You don't need extra periods—just rethink your existing lessons.

Classroom Tools to Promote Skill Building

Tool	Use
Exit slips	Ask a reflective or creative question at the end of class
Student portfolios	Collect evidence of skill use over time
Group reflection	After group work, discuss what went well or could improve
Rubrics	Use simple rubrics to evaluate skills like teamwork or clarity
Peer feedback	Students give structured feedback to each other

Note: These tools take little time but give big results.

Checklist: Are You Nurturing 21st-Century Skills?

Yes/No	Practice
	I ask open-ended or problem-solving questions regularly
	I assign group work with shared responsibilities
	I encourage students to reflect on their learning
	I give students voice in class decisions or discussions
	I assess more than just right/wrong answers

If you answered "yes" to 3 or more—you're helping students prepare for the real world!

DO'S AND DON'TS FOR TEACHING 21st-CENTURY SKILLS

DO	DON'T
Encourage curiosity and challenge students to think	Focus only on textbook content
Allow failure as part of learning	Punish mistakes harshly
Provide flexible tasks with more than one right answer	Only teach for exams or memory
Use student-led discussions	Be the only speaker in class
Build values like respect, resilience, teamwork	Ignore soft skills or feelings

Real-Life Example

A Class 6 science teacher gives this task:
"Create your own invention to solve a problem in your home or school."

Students:

- Brainstorm ideas in groups
- Draw or model their invention
- Present it to the class
- Reflect on what was easy, hard, and fun

Outcomes:

- Critical thinking
- Creativity
- Teamwork
- Communication
- Joyful learning!

Reflective Journal Prompt

- Which 21st-century skill do I already encourage well?
- Which one do I want to focus on next week?
- How can I turn one regular lesson into a skill-building opportunity?

Chapter Summary

- NEP 2020 emphasizes 21st-century skills: critical thinking, creativity, communication, and collaboration
- Skills are not extra—they are part of everyday subject teaching
- Use open-ended questions, group work, reflection, and real-life tasks
- Assess skills through rubrics, peer feedback, and portfolios
- Help students become not just good learners—but smart thinkers and doers

Chapter 11

Classroom Management with Empathy

Objective of the Chapter

To help teachers manage classrooms with empathy, understanding, and inclusion—as encouraged by NEP 2020—while promoting discipline, mutual respect, and joyful learning.

Let's Begin: Managing Minds, Not Just Minutes

Many teachers say, "I can't teach until I control the class." But what if we reframe classroom management not as control, but as connection?

NEP 2020 promotes classrooms that are safe, inclusive, and joyful. That starts with the teacher-student relationship. Empathy—the ability to understand and respect what children feel—is the foundation.

Discipline is important, but it should come from mutual respect, not fear.

What Is Classroom Management?

It means creating a space where:
- Learning can happen without constant interruptions
- Students feel heard, respected, and engaged
- The teacher balances authority with empathy
- Everyone knows the rules and feels safe following them

Good management is not about strict rules—it's about consistent routines and respectful relationships.

Why Empathy Matters

Without Empathy	With Empathy
Students fear the teacher	Students trust the teacher
Misbehavior increases	Children feel safe and listen
One-size-fits-all punishments	Understanding individual needs
Low participation	Confidence and involvement grow

5 Empathetic Strategies for Managing the Classroom

1. Set Clear, Simple Rules Together
Involve students in making classroom rules. This creates ownership.
Try This: "What kind of classroom do we want?"

Let students suggest rules like:
- Listen when someone is speaking
- Keep hands and feet to yourself
- Help friends who need support

2. Use Routines, Not Reactions
Children thrive with predictable structure.

Create a daily routine for:

- Entry and exit
- Transitions between subjects
- Group work
- Asking questions

This reduces confusion and keeps energy focused.

3. Catch Them Being Good

Notice and appreciate positive behavior more than you punish the negative.

Example: "I loved how you waited your turn—well done!"
Praise publicly. Correct privately.

4. Use 'I' Messages Instead of Commands

Instead of "Stop making noise!",

try:
"I feel distracted when there's noise. Can we try to lower our voices?"
This is respectful and teaches emotional awareness.

5. Create a Safe Space for Emotions

Allow children to express feelings through:

- Morning check-ins ("How are you feeling today?")
- Emotion charts
- Quiet corners to calm down

NEP Tip: Joyful learning happens when children feel safe emotionally.

TRY THIS: Daily 10-Minute Connection Plan

Time	Task	Purpose
5 min	Morning circle	Share feelings, thoughts, a story
2 min	Movement break	Release energy between subjects
2 min	Praise highlight	Appreciate one act of kindness or learning
1 min	End-of-day reflection	What did you enjoy today?

A little connection each day builds trust and reduces disruptions.

Checklist: Am I Managing with Empathy?

Yes/No	Practice
	I involve students in setting rules
	I listen to the child's side before reacting
	I praise students for effort and kindness
	I use gentle language to correct behavior
	I create space for children to express emotions

If you answered "yes" to 3 or more—you are building a respectful and safe classroom!

Sample Responses to Common Situations

Situation	Traditional Response	Empathetic Response
A child forgets homework	"Why didn't you bring it again?"	"Is something bothering you? Want to talk?"
Two children are arguing	"Both of you stop now!"	"Let's take turns. One person speaks, then the other."

A student refuses to participate	"If you don't answer, I'll call your parents."	"Would you like to try in a group first?"

Understanding Behavior: It's Communication

Children don't always have the words to express stress, fear, or boredom—so they act out.

Instead of asking:
"What's wrong with this child?"

Ask:
"What's happening to this child?"

Look for triggers:
- Are they hungry, tired, or anxious?
- Is the content too hard?
- Do they need movement or quiet time?

DO'S AND DON'TS FOR EMPATHETIC MANAGEMENT

DO	DON'T
Use calm, clear voice	Shout or threaten
Address behavior, not the child	Say hurtful things like "You're bad"
Offer choices	Force obedience
Give chances to try again	Use strict punishments for small mistakes
Build trust slowly	Expect instant change in difficult students

Mindfulness Tools for Calm Classrooms

Use quick strategies to reduce stress:
• Breathing exercises ("Smell the flower, blow the candle")
• Short body stretches
• Listening to calming sounds or music
• One-minute silence to reset focus
Even 2–3 minutes of mindfulness can prevent bigger disruptions.

Reflective Journal Prompt

• Which child challenges me the most—and why?
• Have I tried understanding their needs or triggers?
• What new strategy can I try this week to connect, not confront?

Chapter Summary

• NEP 2020 encourages respectful, inclusive, and emotionally safe classrooms
• Classroom management should come from empathy, not fear
• Use routines, soft correction, praise, and student voice
• Understand that behavior is often a sign of unmet needs
• A well-managed class is one where children feel seen, safe, and supported

Chapter 12

Gender Sensitivity & Inclusive Education

Objective of the Chapter

To help teachers create gender-sensitive, inclusive classrooms in line with NEP 2020 values, where every child—regardless of gender, ability, or background—feels respected, safe, and able to learn fully.

Let's Begin: Every Child, Every Right

Look around your classroom. Do all your students feel equally seen, heard, and valued?

NEP 2020 focuses on equity, inclusion, and respect for diversity. It reminds us that classrooms must reflect fairness and dignity for all—across gender, caste, language, ability, and background.

And it starts with us—the teachers.

What Is Gender Sensitivity?

Gender sensitivity means understanding that:

• Boys and girls may face different challenges and pressures

• Learning is affected by social expectations (e.g., "Boys don't cry," "Girls are quiet")

• All genders must get equal encouragement, opportunities, and visibility

It's not just about "treating everyone the same"—it's about understanding their realities and responding with fairness.

What Is Inclusive Education?

Inclusive education means ensuring that:

• Children with disabilities, learning differences, or social disadvantages are fully part of the class

• The curriculum, classroom, and assessment adapt to children's needs

• Learning happens in a space of belonging, not isolation

Inclusion is not a "special programme"—it's everyone learning together, with support.

Why It Matters

Inclusive & Gender-Sensitive Class	**Traditional Class**
All children participate freely	Some dominate; others stay silent
Children feel accepted and safe	Some children feel judged or excluded
Learning is joyful and shared	Stress, silence, and fear grow
Prepares children for real world	Promotes stereotypes and divisions

NEP Tip: The curriculum must promote respect for gender, inclusion, empathy, and constitutional values.

5 Simple Ways to Make Your Class More Inclusive and Gender-Sensitive

1. Use Neutral Language

Avoid phrases like:

- "Boys, stop running around!"
- "Girls are better at writing."

Say instead:

- "Let's all walk calmly."
- "Who'd like to share next?" (without choosing by gender)

2. Rotate Responsibilities

Give class roles like line leader, monitor, board cleaner, or group captain to all genders, including shy students and children with disabilities.

Try This: Make a weekly role rotation chart.

3. Use Inclusive Teaching Materials

Check if your textbooks and examples reflect:

- Girls as scientists, pilots, or leaders
- Boys expressing emotions or helping at home
- Children with disabilities achieving goals

Add stories, pictures, and real-life examples that reflect all kinds of children.

4. Celebrate Differences

Mark days and projects around:

- International Day of Persons with Disabilities
- Girl Child Day
- Local language festivals

Let students talk about their identities, homes, and heroes.

5. Support, Don't Separate
If a child needs help (e.g., uses a wheelchair, has dyslexia, or needs language support), give it within the classroom.

Examples:
- Use larger print handouts
- Pair them with a buddy
- Repeat or simplify instructions without drawing attention

TRY THIS: Activities for Inclusion and Awareness

Activity	Purpose
"Same and Different" game	Helps students notice common feelings, even across differences
Role reversal day	Girls and boys switch typical roles (e.g., in drama, sports)
"My Hero" presentations	Let students share diverse role models
Buddy system	Each student helps a peer with reading, movement, or organizing materials
Picture sorting	Show images of people in different roles—discuss stereotypes and facts

These build empathy, awareness, and connection.

Checklist: Is My Classroom Inclusive and Gender-Sensitive?

Yes/No	Practice
	I encourage boys and girls equally to speak and lead

	I include stories/images of people with diverse abilities and roles
	I avoid language that stereotypes any group
	I support children who need extra help without isolating them
	I treat differences (language, dress, culture) with respect and curiosity

3 or more "yes"? You're building an inclusive, NEP-aligned classroom!

DO'S AND DON'TS FOR INCLUSION & GENDER SENSITIVITY

DO	DON'T
Respect names, pronouns, and preferences	Make jokes about gender or background
Give equal time and attention	Ignore quiet or struggling children
Adapt your teaching to diverse needs	Assume one method works for all
Encourage sharing of diverse experiences	Dismiss cultural, religious, or social identity
Promote collaboration over competition	Rank students harshly or create shame

Real-Life Example

In a Class 5 social science class, the teacher noticed only boys were raising their hands.

She changed her strategy:

• Created a "talking stick" to take turns
• Made smaller discussion circles
• Asked children to write answers first, then share aloud

Results:
• Girls and quieter children participated more
• Students listened more respectfully
• Learning felt fair and calm

Reflective Journal Prompt

• Are all children participating in my class—equally and meaningfully?
• What language or behavior might make some feel excluded?
• What's one change I can make this week to promote fairness and belonging?

Chapter Summary

• NEP 2020 calls for inclusive, respectful, gender-sensitive classrooms
• Inclusion is not about separation—it's about support within the group
• Teachers must use language, materials, and strategies that reflect diversity
• Small steps—like rotating roles or changing phrases—build big impact
• Every child has the right to feel safe, valued, and seen

Chapter 13

Making Lessons Joyful and Child-Centric

Objective of the Chapter

To help teachers plan and deliver lessons that are joyful, interactive, and centered on the needs, interests, and experiences of children, as emphasized in NEP 2020.

Let's Begin: Are Children Happy to Learn?

Think about your classroom. Do your students arrive with curiosity or fear? Are your lessons full of laughter, surprise, and discovery? NEP 2020 reminds us that education must be joyful, engaging, and child-centric. Children learn best when they are emotionally connected, not just intellectually stimulated.

A joyful classroom is not noisy chaos—it's a place where students feel free, focused, and involved.

What Does "Child-Centric" Really Mean?

It means:

- Teaching from the child's point of view
- Building on what the child already knows or feels
- Allowing choice, creativity, and voice
- Connecting lessons to real life, not just the textbook

It's not about more entertainment. It's about more meaning.

What Makes a Lesson Joyful?

Element	Why It Works
Stories	Activate imagination and memory
Games	Make learning fun, active, and social
Visuals	Support understanding beyond words
Music, rhythm	Improve focus and retention
Real-world tasks	Help children see the "why" behind learning

Even small changes in delivery can make big changes in engagement.

5 Ways to Add Joy and Meaning to Any Lesson

1. Start with a Hook

Begin with something surprising:

- **A question:** "What would happen if the sun disappeared for a day?"
- **A prop:** Show a leaf, a newspaper, or a simple tool
- **A quick challenge:** "Name 5 things in 10 seconds that float."

The first 3 minutes decide the mood of your class!

2. Use Stories and Real-Life Links

Every concept can be told through a story—personal, historical, or imaginary.

Teaching gravity? Tell the story of Newton and the apple.
Teaching decimals? Use a story about shopping for sweets.

3. Involve the Senses

Children learn better when they see, touch, hear, and move.

Use:

- Role play for dialogue or history
- Leaf collection for science
- Math with bottle caps, sticks, or chalk
- Action songs for younger learners

4. Give Choice and Voice

Offer options:

- "Do you want to draw this or write about it?"
- "Choose your partner or group name."
- "What question do you have about this topic?"

Children love ownership. It builds confidence and interest.

5. Celebrate Effort, Not Just Results

Use praise, stickers, "star of the day," and positive notes for:

- Trying something new
- Helping a friend
- Asking a brave question

Joy grows when children feel safe, supported, and seen.

TRY THIS: A Joyful Lesson Routine (35–40 minutes)

Time	What to Do	Purpose
5 min	Warm-up (riddle, song, movement)	Activate curiosity
10 min	Main concept (story, visual, object)	Teach through meaning

10 min	Activity (group task, drawing, matching)	Learn by doing
5 min	Sharing and reflection	Student voice and learning
5 min	Closure with praise or a fun question	Build joy and memory

Ideas by Subject

Subject	Joyful Strategy
English	Puppet storytelling, poem recitation circles
Math	Number line games, real object grouping
Science	Hands-on experiments, nature walks
Social Science	Timelines with drawings, community interviews
Languages	Tongue twisters, vocabulary bingo
Art	Combine subjects with sketching and colouring

Checklist: Am I Making My Class Joyful?

Yes/No	Practice
	I include at least one interactive task in every lesson
	I allow children to speak, choose, and reflect
	I use real-life connections or props
	I praise effort and ideas, not just correct answers

	I smile, move around, and enjoy the class with my students

If you ticked 3 or more, you're spreading learning joy!

DO'S AND DON'TS FOR A CHILD-CENTRIC CLASSROOM

DO	DON'T
Connect lessons to what children already know	Teach only from the textbook
Encourage mistakes as learning steps	Scold for wrong answers harshly
Involve all learning styles (visual, auditory, kinesthetic)	Use only lectures or blackboard notes
Allow students to talk and move (with purpose)	Demand silence all the time
Ask, listen, and adapt	Deliver content without checking interest

Real-Life Example

A Class 2 teacher turned a lesson on hygiene into a story about "Toothbrush Warrior" who defeats sugar bugs.

Children:

- Drew their own superhero tools
- Shared brushing songs
- Taught the story at home

Result: Joyful recall + real-life habit-building!

Reflective Journal Prompt

- Which part of my last lesson made students smile or engage most?
- Did I allow children to express or create?
- What's one joyful change I'll try in tomorrow's class?

Chapter Summary

- NEP 2020 promotes joyful, discovery-based, and child-centered learning
- Start with curiosity, build through activity, and end with reflection
- Use stories, games, movement, and student voice
- Praise effort and create a space where children feel excited to learn
- When children enjoy learning, they learn better—and remember longer

Chapter 14

Working with Parents & Community

Objective of the Chapter

To help teachers build strong, collaborative relationships with parents and the local community as equal partners in a child's learning journey, in line with NEP 2020's vision of a school-family-community ecosystem.

Let's Begin: School Is Not an Island

Children don't learn in school alone. They learn at home, in parks, through festivals, from elders, and by observing the world around them.

NEP 2020 recognizes that parents and community members are key partners in education. When teachers, families, and communities work together, students feel supported, connected, and more motivated.

The goal is not to inform parents after a term ends—it's to engage them from the start.

Why Parents Matter in a Child's Learning

Involved Parents	Disconnected Parents
Monitor learning at home	Rely entirely on school
Understand child's needs	Feel left out and helpless
Partner in problem-solving	Blame school or stay silent
Support attendance and discipline	Miss early warning signs

Students do better—academically, emotionally, and socially—when home and school work together.

Why Community Matters

Your school is part of a living community full of:
• Local knowledge (farmers, shopkeepers, artisans)
• Culture and tradition (festivals, music, dress)
• Resources (parks, museums, leaders, libraries)

NEP 2020 encourages schools to bring the outside world in—and to take students into the world.

5 Practical Ways to Partner with Parents

1. Start Positive, Stay Consistent
Don't wait for a problem to contact parents. Share positive feedback early.

Tip: A short message like "Priya helped a friend today" can build lasting goodwill.

2. Host Friendly, Structured PTMs (Parent-Teacher Meetings)
Replace "report card lectures" with conversations.

Suggested PTM Format:

- **5 mins:** Warm welcome and overview
- **10 mins:** Child's strengths (academic + personal)
- **5 mins:** Area for growth + how school/home can support
- **5 mins:** Questions and suggestions from parents

Use simple charts, samples of work, or even student self-assessments.

3. Create Two-Way Communication Channels

Use WhatsApp groups (with clear rules), diaries, phone calls, or short video messages.

Make space for parents to share updates too—e.g., "Amit started reading a storybook this week!"

4. Involve Parents in Learning

Invite parents to:

- Tell stories or folk songs
- Demonstrate local crafts or farming tools
- Judge competitions or be audience members
- Share their career journeys (driver, nurse, artist—all matter!)

This shows children that learning happens everywhere, and parents feel included.

5. Respect Their Context

Not all parents can read or attend meetings. Some may work long hours. Be inclusive.

Tips:

- Offer audio updates instead of written
- Meet in community spaces or weekends
- Send visuals, not just text

Community Connections You Can Build

Activity	Community Link
Nature walk	Local garden or farm
Heritage day	Village elders, artisans
Health talk	Local nurse or doctor
Cleanliness drive	Panchayat members or municipal staff
Tree planting	Forest officer or community volunteers

NEP Tip: Learning must connect to local culture, environment, and economy.

TRY THIS: Parent Feedback Form Template (Simple)

Child's Name:
Class & Section:
Date:

1. What progress have you seen in your child this term?
[Open space for answer]

2. What is one thing you'd like the teacher to know about your child?
[Open space for answer]

3. How can we support you better?
[Tick boxes]
More communication
Home learning tips
Flexible meeting times

Other: __________
Signature:

Checklist: Am I Partnering with Parents?

Yes/No	Practice
	I contact parents for positive updates—not just complaints
	I listen to parents' concerns with empathy
	I plan PTMs to be short, friendly, and useful
	I invite parents to participate in class or school events
	I adapt my communication to suit different parent needs

If you ticked 3 or more, you're building a strong school-home bridge!

DO'S AND DON'TS FOR PARENT & COMMUNITY PARTNERSHIPS

DO	DON'T
Treat parents as partners, not problems	Talk down or blame
Appreciate local knowledge and culture	Ignore or look down on non-academic skills
Use respectful tone and flexible methods	Expect every parent to read/ write fluently
Encourage sharing, questions, and ideas	Make communication one-sided
Connect lessons to real-life and local life	Teach only from textbook examples

Real-Life Example

A Class 4 teacher in rural Maharashtra invited a student's grandmother—an expert in millet recipes—to demonstrate healthy cooking.

Children:

• Learned about local grains
• Asked questions in their mother tongue
• Connected science with daily life

Parents saw their knowledge valued. Children saw school as relevant.

Reflective Journal Prompt

• When was the last time I contacted a parent with good news?
• How many parents have I personally spoken to this term?
• What new way can I include the community in one lesson next month?

Chapter Summary

• NEP 2020 encourages school-family-community partnerships for holistic learning
• Communicate early, often, and respectfully with parents
• Include parents in the learning process—not just in exams
• Use local community knowledge to enrich your lessons
• When homes and schools work together, children thrive

Chapter 15

The Reflective Teacher

Your Self-Improvement Journal

Objective of the Chapter

To encourage teachers to reflect regularly on their teaching practices, identify strengths and growth areas, and continuously improve themselves as lifelong learners, in alignment with NEP 2020's emphasis on professional development and inner transformation.

Let's Begin: Learning Doesn't End with the Teacher

In every classroom, the teacher teaches—and the teacher learns. NEP 2020 envisions every educator as a reflective practitioner: someone who doesn't just deliver lessons but also regularly pauses, thinks, and improves their methods, mindset, and outcomes.

Reflection is not a luxury. It's the fuel for professional growth and student success.

What Is Reflective Teaching?

Reflective teaching is the habit of asking yourself:
• What went well in my class today?
• What didn't work—and why?
• What can I do differently tomorrow?

It helps you:
• Understand your students better
• Adjust your strategies
• Reduce stress
• Improve outcomes

Think of it as a mirror—not for judgment, but for clarity.

Why Reflective Practice Matters

Without Reflection	With Reflection
Repeating the same mistakes	Learning from experience
Feeling stuck or tired	Feeling aware and purposeful
Blaming students or conditions	Taking ownership and making change
Teaching for completion	Teaching for impact

5 Practical Ways to Become a Reflective Teacher

1. Use the "3-1" Method After Every Class

Ask yourself:
• What are 3 things that went well?
• What is 1 thing I want to improve?

Example:
Students enjoyed the group activity

I managed time well
I used real-life examples
Need to ask more open-ended questions next time
Write it in a notebook or phone at the end of the day.

2. Maintain a Weekly Reflection Journal

Reserve 15 minutes each weekend to write about:

- Your favorite class this week—and why
- A student who challenged you—and what you learned
- A teaching technique you want to try

Over time, this builds a map of your progress.

3. Set Personal Teaching Goals

Your goals could be:

- "I want to reduce my blackboard use and include more visual aids."
- "I will call out at least 2 positive behaviors each day."

Keep goals small, specific, and trackable.

4. Seek Feedback

Ask your students:

- "What did you enjoy in this topic?"
- "What confused you the most?"
- "How do you want to learn this next time?"

Ask peers to observe your class and share thoughts.
Learning happens faster when we learn from each other.

5. Celebrate Growth

Reflect not just on what went wrong—but on how far you've come.

Look back every 3 months and ask:

- What strategies now feel easy, but didn't before?
- Which students improved because of something I did?

Growth may be slow, but it's always happening if we notice it.

Sample Journal Entry Format

Date:
Class/Topic:

What went well today?
1.
2.
3.

What can I improve?
1.

What will I try next time?
Mood of the class:
Mood of the teacher:

Reflection Prompts for Teachers

Use these weekly or monthly:

Prompt	Purpose
"What's one moment I felt proud this week?"	Celebrating success
"What drained my energy most?"	Identifying burnout triggers
"Which student surprised me—and how?"	Deepening relationships
"What new technique did I try?"	Tracking innovation
"What help do I need from my peers or leader?"	Asking for support

Checklist: Am I a Reflective Educator?

Yes/No	Practice
	I take time weekly to think about my teaching
	I write or record my reflections
	I try new ideas based on what I learn
	I ask for feedback from students or peers
	I celebrate small wins and effort, not just outcomes

If you checked 3 or more—you are on your journey to becoming a NEP-aligned, self-aware teacher.

DO'S AND DON'TS OF REFLECTIVE TEACHING

DO	DON'T
Reflect regularly	Wait for end-of-year reviews
Be honest, but kind to yourself	Blame yourself harshly
Write it down or record voice notes	Keep everything in your head
Act on your insights	Reflect but never change
Enjoy the journey	Expect overnight transformation

Real-Life Example

A middle school teacher in Delhi began journaling twice a week.

In her entries, she noticed:
- She always felt rushed on Tuesdays
- Group work went better when she assigned specific roles
- She was often too tired by Friday to enjoy teaching

She made two small changes:

- Introduced visual lesson starters on Tuesdays
- Took 10 minutes for music or storytelling on Fridays

Her engagement—and the students'—improved dramatically.

Reflective Journal Prompt

- What kind of teacher do I want to be 6 months from now?
- What is one area I want to grow in—and why?
- What is the next small step I can take this week?

Chapter Summary

- NEP 2020 encourages teachers as lifelong learners and reflective practitioners
- Reflection helps improve teaching quality, confidence, and connection with students
- Simple methods like the 3-1 technique, weekly journals, and feedback loops work best
- Growth is personal, ongoing, and deeply rewarding
- A reflective teacher is a resilient, responsive, and respected educator

Glossary of Key NEP 2020 Terms

A

Active Learning
A method where students engage directly in activities like discussion, problem-solving, or role play rather than passive listening.
Assessment for Learning
A type of ongoing, formative assessment used to guide future teaching and improve learning—rather than only judge it.

B

Blended Learning
A teaching approach that combines traditional face-to-face classroom methods with digital or online tools and content.
Bridge Language
The familiar language used by a teacher to connect a child's home language to the medium of instruction (often English or Hindi).

C

Child-Centric Learning
A classroom approach that focuses on the interests, needs, and pace of the child rather than the curriculum or teacher's plan alone.
Competency-Based Education
Education that focuses on mastering specific learning outcomes (skills or concepts), rather than completing fixed hours or chapters.
Continuous Professional Development (CPD)
Ongoing training and self-improvement opportunities for teachers to update and upgrade their teaching practices and knowledge.

D

DIKSHA

Digital Infrastructure for Knowledge Sharing – A national online platform for teachers and students offering free learning content and courses.

Discovery-Based Learning

An approach where students learn by exploring, investigating, and finding answers themselves, often through real-life tasks or experiments.

E

Experiential Learning

Learning through hands-on experiences—doing, reflecting, and applying knowledge to real-life situations.

Early Childhood Care and Education (ECCE)

Education and care for children from 0 to 8 years, focusing on physical, social, emotional, and cognitive development.

F

Foundational Literacy and Numeracy (FLN)

Basic ability to read with understanding and do basic math. The foundation for all future learning; a top priority of NEP 2020.

Formative Assessment

Assessment done during the learning process to give feedback, not just to grade. Helps improve teaching and student understanding.

H

Holistic Progress Card (HPC)

A report card that reflects overall growth—academic performance, co-curricular skills, socio-emotional development, and values.

I

Inclusive Education

Education that includes all learners—regardless of ability, language, or background—by removing barriers and offering support.

Inquiry-Based Learning

An approach that begins with a question, not an answer. Encourages curiosity, critical thinking, and problem-solving.

J

Joyful Learning

Learning that makes children happy, engaged, and interested—through songs, games, stories, and discovery.

L

Learning Outcomes

Clearly defined skills, knowledge, or attitudes a student should gain after a lesson or unit. These guide teaching and assessment.

Lifelong Learning

The idea that learning doesn't stop after school or college—it continues throughout life and across all ages.

M

Multilingual Education

A system that allows students to learn in their mother tongue while gradually acquiring other languages like English or Hindi.

Mother Tongue/Home Language

The language most spoken by a child at home. NEP suggests using this as the medium of instruction at early grades.

N

NEP 2020
National Education Policy 2020 – India's education reform policy aiming to make learning holistic, flexible, inclusive, and skill-oriented.
NISHTHA
National Initiative for School Heads' and Teachers' Holistic Advancement – India's largest teacher training programme under NEP.

P

Portfolio Assessment
A collection of a student's work over time that shows progress and creativity—used as an assessment method.
Play-Based Learning
Learning through structured and unstructured play—especially effective in foundational and preparatory stages.

R

Reflective Practice
The habit of regularly thinking about and improving one's teaching practice through self-review or journaling.
Remedial Learning
Additional learning support provided to students who are falling behind to help them meet learning goals.

S

Scaffolding
Temporary support provided by the teacher (like hints, prompts, or examples) to help students achieve learning tasks independently.
Student Agency

Empowering students to make choices in their learning—what they learn, how they learn, and how they express it.

T

Toy-Based Pedagogy

Use of toys, games, and traditional play items to promote interactive and meaningful learning, especially in early years.

Transdisciplinary Learning

Integrating knowledge from multiple subjects into a single project or theme, to reflect how learning occurs in real life.

V

Vocational Education

Practical skill-based education that prepares students for careers in trades or jobs, introduced from Grade 6 under NEP.